M000107417

Casherific Money Managing Activities

by Molly McMahon

Editorial: Aimee Hansen, Kristy Kugler, Paul Rawlins
Art and Design: Andy Carlson, Robyn Funk, Magen Mitchell, Amanda Sorensen

ISBN 1-59441-722-9

Reasons for Working

When you were very young, everything you needed appeared like *magic*. You had tasty food, bubbly baths, exciting toys, and colorful books. Now that you are older you know that someone had to buy the food, pay for the hot water, and shop for the toys and books. That someone was probably your mom or dad. However, soon that someone will be you!

Do you ask your mom for a quarter every time you pass a gum ball machine? Do you dream of the latest video game or a ticket to a concert? Having spending money is a good reason to work. Having your own money to save and spend as you wish is worth the time it takes to do a job.

Trying out the different jobs in this book will teach you a lot about yourself. Have you ever weeded a garden? You might find you like beautiful flowers. Great! The world is looking for young scientists to develop plants that can feed the poor and hungry. You might like children, but once you try "mommy sitting" you might find that changing a dirty diaper is just not your thing. A job is like a new food someone wants you to taste: until you take a bite you can't really say if you like it or not. So, go ahead and try a job. You might like it!

MONEY TIP: A good time to start leaning how to make, spend, and save money is when you are in elementary school.

I'm Just a Kid! What Can I Do?

The best way to start making money is to get to know yourself better. Make a list of things you like. Make another list of all the things you know how to do, no matter how silly they might seem. You will be amazed by how long your list is. Look at the example below. Your list will be much longer.

SKILLS I HAVE
shooting free throws
baking muffins
filling bird feeders
cleaning up after my dog

THINGS I LIKE
basketball
cooking
animals

Skills I Have

_____

_____

_____

_____

_____

_____

_____

Things I Like

_____

_____

_____

_____

_____

_____

_____

Add to your list as you develop new likes and skills.

> "A single idea—the sudden flash of thought—
> may be worth a million dollars."
> —Robert Collier

Activity

1

Piggy Spends/Piggy Saves

MONEY TIP: By the year 2015 it may cost more than $25,000 a year to attend a 4-year public university. How old will you be in 2015? Start **now** to save for college.

Economists (ee-kon-oh-mists) are people who study how people use money, goods, and natural resources. Economists are worried that young Americans aren't learning to save money. People in the United States save less of what they earn than people in many other countries.

Saving money is an important habit to learn. An education, a home, and a car are all expensive and require some savings to be able to afford them. *Think of it this way: If you earn $1.00 a day and you spend a $1.00 each day, you will never be able to buy anything that costs $2.00! If you want something that costs $2.00, you will need to* **spend less** *than $1.00 each day and* **save up** *until you have the $2.00 you need.*

During the Middle Ages (mid-1500s) people saved their money in earthen pots made from **pygg**. Pygg is a type of orange clay that was found in Europe. Within 200 years, these jars were shaped like pigs, an animal that was a symbol of thrift, or savings. This pygg jar was later called a "piggy bank."

"**A penny saved is a penny earned.**"
—**Benjamin Franklin**

Two Piggy Jars

Keep two different money jars in your room. It doesn't matter what your jars look like. Nowadays, piggy banks come in all sorts of shapes and sizes. The important idea is that you know which one is your Spending Piggy and which one is your Savings Piggy.

Spending Piggy—The money in this piggy can be spent on anything you want or need, at any time! Your family may have special rules about what you may buy. Always respect these rules.

Savings Piggy—The money in this piggy is collected for a month. Then it goes directly into your savings account at the bank. (See pages 8–9.) Don't worry how small the amount might be—just get it into the bank. Even pennies can add up to a lot of money over several years. You'll use your savings for big expenses or purchases in the future.

- A calculator can help you figure how much to save.
- A good plan for savings is to save 20% of everything you earn or receive as gifts.
- Here is an example of how to figure out how much 20% is. If you earn $1.00, you would multiply 1.00 by .20, which equals .20, or 20 cents.
  Subtract $.20 from the $1.00 and you get 80 cents.
  80 cents goes into your spending piggy, and 20 cents goes into your savings piggy. It is as simple as that!

Spending Piggy

Savings Piggy

Activity 2

My Social Security Number

MONEY TIP: Some people believe that a penny you find is a "lucky penny" and that you should keep it forever. Tape or glue a lucky penny to your Savings Piggy. Then, put any other pennies you find **inside** the piggy, and at the end of the month take them to the bank.

To start a savings account you need to have your **Social Security card**. *Social* means "group," and *security* means "safety." A Social Security card has a nine-digit number on it that the U.S. government assigns to each of its citizens.

The number looks like this:

555-55-5555

No one else will have the same Social Security number (SSN) as you. You will use the same number for the rest of your life. Your parents or guardian should have the original card.

A Social Security card looks like this:

Memorize Your Number

Parents usually fill out the forms for a Social Security number for a baby before the baby is brought home from the hospital. However, if you have not yet received a SSN, you will need an application to get one. If you are a U.S. citizen, ask a trustworthy adult to help you call 1-800-772-1213 or get a form off the Internet at www.ssa.gov.

- Your Social Security card is an important piece of paper. Keep it in a safe place along with your birth certificate.

- MEMORIZE your Social Security number. Just like knowing your address and phone number, you should know your SSN. You will need it at banks and at schools. Without it, it will be hard to get a driver's license or a job when you become a teenager.

- NEVER tell anyone your Social Security number without your parents' permission. The Internet is a very unsafe place to use this number. Remember, the number is yours and belongs to no one else. As you grow up, your parents will teach you when and where it is safe to use it.

"A rich man is nothing but a poor man with money."
—W. C. Fields

Activity
3

My Own Savings Account

MONEY TIP: Find a bank near your home where you can open a savings account. The farther away a bank is from your house, the less likely you will make monthly deposits. A **deposit** is something you put in a bank or safe place.

People who own banks tell other people to "*Put your money to work!*" If you have worked hard selling lemonade or picking apples up off the ground, the idea of something else doing the work sounds pretty good.

The big question is: "How can I make my money work for me?"

The big answer is: "Put money in a savings account, and it will work to make more money!"

When you put money into a savings account and keep it there, the bank will pay you money, called **interest**. Each day the bank adds a little bit of money to your money. You don't have to do a thing! Here is a very simple example:

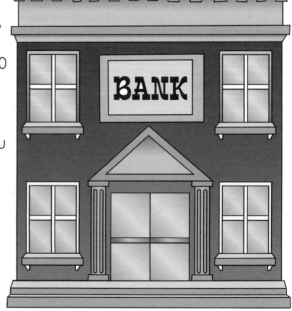

Suppose the bank pays you 3% interest a year on your savings. Next, pretend you have $100.00 in savings. $100 x .03 = $3.00! If you leave the $100 in your piggy bank, it will still be worth $100 at the end of a year. If you put the $100 to work in a savings account, it will be worth $103 after a year.

Finding a Bank

In Mexico, the Aztecs and Mayans used transparent bird quills filled with gold dust and cloth sacks containing exactly 24,000 cocoa beans for money. Taking your coins and paper bills to a bank has to be easier than counting out that many cocoa beans!

Picking the best bank for your savings account will take some research. Use the Yellow Pages or business section of your local telephone book to find some choices. Some banks offer "student accounts." Some banks require that a parent or guardian open the account along with you. Some banks that offer what you want might be far from your home. Others might not be the best, but are closer. Talk with your parents and ask them to help you decide. Then, go to the New Accounts desk at the bank you have chosen and ask for the forms you need.

- Take your Social Security card and birth certificate or picture ID with you to the bank.
- Fill the forms out in non-erasable pen.
- Keep your savings account number in a safe place.
- Return both your Social Security card and birth certificate to a safe place.

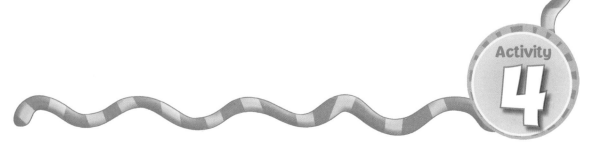

Activity

4

It's a Dog's World

> **MONEY TIP:** Whenever you get coins as payment for a job or as change at a store, take a few seconds to look carefully at each one. A coin that looks different from others you have seen could be worth a "pretty penny"!

Humans have kept dogs as pets for over 12,000 years. The oldest dog remains in the Americas are from Danger Cave, Utah. They date back to 9,000-10,000 B.C. The **domesticated**, or tame, dog is related to wolves, jackals, foxes, and coyotes.

About 1 in every 3 U.S. families owns a dog. Most dogs live between 8 and 15 years. An Australian sheepdog that lived for over 29 years is listed as the oldest dog.

Humans become very devoted to their dogs. Humans also get busy with jobs or go on vacations and need someone to feed their dogs. Older people sometimes need someone to walk their pet. There are several chores that need to be done to keep a dog healthy and happy: feeding, walking, brushing, and picking up its poop. The next few pages are about jobs dealing with dogs. As long as you are not allergic to "man's best friend," you could consider any of these jobs.

Finding All Dogs

To earn money by caring for a dog, you first need to find the dog. The best dog is one that's close to your house. It doesn't make much sense to drive all the way across a city to feed a dog twice a day. Unless, of course, you live in a small town or are willing to ride a bicycle to the job.

Be nosy! Take a long walk around your neighborhood with a clipboard, paper, and pencil.

- Write down the addresses of homes that have dogs. Use both your eyes and ears. You might not see the dog, but you might *hear* it!
- Ask people who are walking their dogs if they ever need care for their pets. If they say yes, write down their names and addresses. Let them know that you will leave information about your service in their mailbox.
- Next, use the business directory in your local telephone book and call dog kennels. Ask how much they charge for boarding a dog overnight. *If the average cost of overnight care is $20.00, and you offer to care for a dog at $25.00 per day, you probably won't get hired.*
- Many large cities now have "day boarding" for dogs. Just like child daycare, these businesses do dog daycare. Ask what one day of dog care costs and what services that includes.
- Make a list of which dog chores you will do and how much you will ask to be paid. Talk with an adult to see if the amount you want to charge is reasonable.

Activity

5

Dog Walking

> **MONEY TIP:** Be sure you are asking the right amount of money for a job. Some jobs just aren't worth any amount of money. The heaviest, as well as the longest, dog ever recorded was an Old English mastiff named Zorba. In 1989, Zorba weighed 343 pounds and was 8 feet, 3 inches long from the tip of the nose to the tip of the tail. *How much would you charge to walk this dog around the block?*

Farm dogs, or working dogs, don't need to be walked. They get their exercise herding sheep, chasing chickens, or nipping at the feet of wandering cattle. On the other hand, most cities have laws against dogs being off their property without a leash.

A city dog that is kept inside a home or fenced in a small backyard becomes a miserable dog if it is not walked. These dogs often bark at anything that moves. They chew on furniture, shoes, rugs, and tables. They annoy the postal worker or any stranger who appears on the front porch. Usually, they are not bad dogs. They are just dogs that need a nice long walk.

- After you have been hired to walk a dog, ask its owner to go on a short walk with you and the dog. This way you and the dog can get to know each other.
- With the owner present, practice clipping and unclipping the dog leash until you can do it with confidence.
- Check to see if you should take a specific path. Some dogs like to always follow the same route so they can sniff out special smells. Others like to explore.

Dog Brushing

**Q: What kind of dog loves bubble baths?
A: A shampoodle.**

Dogs are hairy—just plain hairy. There are a few breeds of hairless dogs, but these are an exception. Most dogs, even shorthairs, shed plenty of fur, especially in warm weather. Brushing a dog can be a quick and simple job, or it can be very time consuming. It all depends on the pooch's personality and the length of its coat. Charge more for a longhaired dog than a shorthaired dog. Unlike dog walking, dog brushing is only needed once or twice a week.

The only skills you need to be a dog-brusher are patience and the ability to keep a dog calm. If you are allergic to animal fur or are overly bouncy, this is not the job for you.

- Once you have found a dog to brush, set up a time to watch the owner brush the animal. (At your age, never wash a dog alone!)
- Does the owner make certain sounds to calm the dog?
- Do you do its back first and then the stomach? Or stomach and then the back?
- How do you hold the dog's ears while you brush behind them?
- Have a practice session with the dog's owner present before you start doing this job on your own.

Activity
6

Be a Poop Scooper

Don't turn your nose up at this job! In large cities there are grownups making a full-time living scooping up dog poop from yards. There are big bucks in poop.

Why would anyone scoop poop for a living? The answer is simple: Many dog owners just don't have the time to clean up after their pets, or they find the job too smelly. Your dog-loving neighbors will be thrilled when you offer this service.

Materials
rubber gloves
a bucket lined with a plastic bag
a shovel

Directions
1. Put the dog or dogs in the house before you start this job. Someone scooping its poop is very exciting to a dog, and you don't want it knocking you over.
2. Put on the rubber gloves.
3. Use the shovel to place the poop into the bucket lined with the plastic bag.
4. When you are finished, use a hose or faucet to rinse off the shovel.
5. Tie a knot in the plastic bag and toss it into the owner's garbage can.
6. Wash your hands with soap and water at the end of each job.

• The trick to keep from smelling something unpleasant is to breathe through your mouth, not through your nose.

"He who gathers money little by little makes it grow."
—Proverbs 13:11

Dog-Sitting

MONEY TIP: Give potential customers an index card attached to an inexpensive magnet. A full sheet of paper will probably be thrown away. Your index card can be stuck to a refrigerator.

Caring for another person's pet is a big responsibility. A dog is a living creature. Without proper attention, a dog can get ill or even die. If the dog could open a can of food or pour a bowl of fresh water for itself, you wouldn't be hired to dog-sit.

Dog-sitting is different from dog washing, brushing, or poop scooping. The dog's owner is usually not at home. The dog may need a sitter for only one night or several weeks. Never accept a dog-sitting job unless you are available for the entire time. The owner has hired you, not another family member or friend, to take care of the dog.

What to Know

- Where is the food dish and water bowl? How much and how often do you feed the dog?
- Are you responsible for walking the dog? If so, reread **Dog Walking**.
- Are you responsible for cleaning up the backyard? If so, read **Be a Poop Scooper**.
- What is the name and phone number of the dog's vet in case of an emergency?
- How can the dog's owner be contacted in case of an emergency?

Activity

8

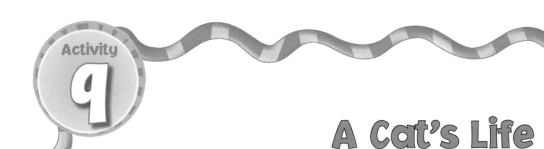

A Cat's Life

MONEY TIP: Know your customer before you hand out an index card offering a certain service. Dog owners aren't looking for cat-sitters, and the grandmother down the street probably does not need a "tot walker." Don't waste your cards or magnets on someone who will just toss them in the trash.

Have you heard this joke? *A dog comes when you call, but a cat takes a message and gets back to you later.* Cats are more independent than dogs. Dogs love to run up to humans. They lick, jump, nuzzle—they'll do anything to get you to notice them. Cats, on the other hand, often slink around corners looking at humans with suspicion. Only when you are still and quiet will they let you pet them. And they certainly don't want to be put on a leash and walked around the block!

Cats can be left several days in a home with a bowl of dry food, a self-watering container, and a litter box. When its owner is gone, a cat will spend most of the time curled up in a ball sleeping. The cat will wake up to eat and drink, maybe play with a ball of catnip or sharpen its nails on a scratching post, then find a new place to sleep.

Another saying states that *thousands of years ago, cats were worshipped as gods, and they have never forgotten that humans were their servants.* You will be hired to put food in the cat's bowl and clean the litter box. If the cat you are sitting lets you rub it behind the ears or bats around a piece of ribbon, consider yourself lucky. You have gotten the attention of a former god or goddess.

More on a Cat's Life

Jack Wright of Kingston, Ontario, is the Guiness world record holder for owning the most cats at one time: 689. Just think how much money you could make cat-sitting for this owner!

Follows these directions for a successful cat-sitting job:

* Get clear directions on filling the cat's bowl with food and where to put it. Cats can be picky and might stop eating if you put the bowl in the wrong spot.
• If the cat gets its water through a self-filling gadget, make sure you know how to refill it.
• Know where the litter box and clean litter is kept. Ask how often the box is to be changed and where to put the dirty litter.
• Cats come in three types: *outdoor only*, *indoor-outdoor*, and *indoor only*. It is important to know which kind of cat you are sitting. Never let an *indoor only* cat sneak out while the door is open. Remember, most cats don't come when you call them.
• If you are sitting an *indoor-outdoor* cat, find out when you should let it in and let it out. If you are lucky, the house will have a "kitty door," and the cat will come and go as it pleases.
• With an *outdoor only* cat, you will only need to feed and water the cat. It most likely will not have a litter box.

A CAT'S MOTTO

**No matter what you've done wrong,
always try to make it look like the dog did it.**

Mommy-Sitting

MONEY TIP: Clearly print the service you are advertising across the top of an index card. Neatness counts! First impressions are important. If the first impression of you is *sloppy*, you might not be hired.

Mommy-sitting is different from *babysitting*. When you *babysit*, the child's parents leave the house. Many states have laws that don't allow parents to leave their children with anyone under the age of 12. *Mommy-sitting* is when you tend children while the parents stay home. It is a job that lasts for one to two hours. A perfect time to be a mommy-sitter is between ages 8 and 12.

With small children at home, it can be hard for moms to find a little quiet time to take a bubble bath, read a book, or finish knitting a sweater. Mommy-sitters let a parent do something at home without being interrupted by their children.

At the same time, the sitter learns important tending skills. Plus, the sitter has the safety of an adult being nearby if there is an emergency.

Pack a Fun Bag

Mark Twain wrote, "My mother had a great deal of trouble with me, but I think she enjoyed it." She must have been a woman who was patient, calm, and even-tempered. If you tend young children, you'll need these qualities.

One of the best ways to prepare for mommy-sitting is to take a class on childcare at a children's hospital. These classes teach lessons on child safety, such as how to avoid poisonings, falling injuries, or drownings. They also teach you how to safely play with infants and toddlers.

- Charge about half of what babysitters in your neighborhood make each hour. The parent is in the house, so you have less responsibility.
- Agree ahead of time on how much you will be paid for each hour. Say, "I charge _____ dollars for every hour I sit. Is that okay with you?"
- DON'T chat on the phone with friends, surf the Internet, do homework, or listen to music with earphones. You are being paid to watch young children, not to amuse yourself.
- If you watch TV or DVDs with the children, make sure that the shows are OK with the parent. Different families have different rules.
- DO bring a bag of fun toys, picture books, and DVDs to your sitting job. Dig around in your basement, closets, and attic to find "new" old toys.

"A mother is a bank where we deposit all our hurts and worries."
—T. DeWitt Talmage

Activity

10

Walk a Tot

MONEY TIP: A **reference** is someone who knows you well and is willing to tell someone else about your abilities and good character. Talk to the person you would like to have be a reference for you. Ask if it's okay for customers to call and chat about you. At the bottom of your index cards write:

For reference, call _person's name_ at _person's telephone number_.

Children between 18 months and 6 years old seem to have two levels of activity: asleep and on the go. Parents can be worn to a frazzle trying to keep up with youngsters. A toddler will hold his mother's hand, dragging her here and there as he explores the world. A four-year-old will skip along a sidewalk daring her father to catch her. Sometimes, it seems like children never stop.

Little children need lots of physical activity. Without exercise, they get cranky and mischievous. A wise woman once said, "The best cure for a short temper is a long walk." Many parents would jump with joy knowing that a responsible youth would take their child outside for a *long walk.*

Looking at the World Upside Down

A walk around a city block is an adventure to most toddlers. But it takes patience not to hurry. The distance you might walk in 5 minutes could take 30 minutes with a three-year-old. Small children are learning from everything around them, and their natural interest in exploring is healthy. Here is a list of things to think about before you begin a *walking service*.

- Make sure the child has the correct type of shoes. The shoes should have closed toes and heels to protect the child's feet from broken glass, sharp rocks, or gravel.
- If rain is in the forecast, have an umbrella for each person on the walk. Children often love to walk in the rain as long as it's not too cold.
- Small children get cold easily, so remember hats and gloves in chilly weather.
- All year long, use sunblock on exposed skin.
- If there is high wind or loud thunder, return home immediately.
- Be patient! Touch, smell, and carefully examine every little item the child points out. They are curious, and you are the teacher.
- If the child looks upside down at something, do the same. The world certainly seems different when you are looking through your legs.

"Remember, when children have a tantrum, don't have one of your own."
—Dr. Judith Kuriansky

Activity

11

Activity 12

Party Helper

> **MONEY TIP:** Discuss the idea of an **allowance** with your parents. An allowance is a sum of money given to you at regular times to be used as you choose. *If your parents are not willing to give you an allowance, be respectful of their reasons.*

A *host* (male) or *hostess* (female) is a person who invites people to a party.

The time before, during, and after a party can be very busy. The host usually wants to be with the guests. He does not want to be busy making sure everyone has something to eat. And the thought of a messy kitchen after the guests have gone home can make a hostess think twice about giving a party at all!

What this means is a host or hostess often could use some extra help. A party helper is a great job to do with a friend. It is a service that could become a huge hit in your neighborhood. When word gets out that you are willing to help at everything from a birthday party for a bunch of five-year-olds to a fancy party for adults, your phone could ring constantly.

Dress in Black and White

When you work as a party helper, dress in a special way so people can tell who you are. At restaurants, you often see servers wearing black and white. Dig around in your closet and come up with a party helper uniform. A white shirt or blouse and a pair of black pants make a good uniform. Your outfit should be spotlessly clean and ironed. If you help at a fancy party, such as an anniversary dinner or an outdoor summer celebration, ask if there is a color theme. Then you can add a tie or hair ribbon to your uniform to match.

Here are some things a party helper might do:
• Serve pre-dinner snacks to guests.
• Serve plates to the guests and clear away the dishes when empty. (Always serve a full plate over the guest's right arm and clear an empty plate over the guest's left arm).
• Wash dishes and stack them on a table for the hostess to put away later.
• Be a "lifeguard" at a children's swim party. You would be an extra pair of eyes watching the pool and keeping children from running or diving off edges. A black swimsuit or a swimsuit with a pin that says "Junior Lifeguard" on it could take the place of the white shirt and black pants.
• Walk children from door to door on Halloween.
• Make your own list of party helper ideas.

_____

_____

_____

_____

"Ideas are the beginning points of fortunes."
—Napoleon Hill

Activity
12

The Care of Garbage Cans

MONEY TIP: Offer to do household chores for an allowance. Some parents will give their children an allowance if they are willing to learn job skills. Make a contract that clearly states what jobs you are doing, what the payment will be, and when the jobs are to be completed.

It will not be your parents' responsibility to remind you of your chores. If you don't do them on time, agree that you won't be paid.

Can you think of a time when someone offered you a dollar to eat a piece of delicious, homemade chocolate cake? Do any of your friends get paid to go to Disneyland? Do you get an allowance for having a snowball war with your brothers or hanging around the swimming pool with your schoolmates? The answer to all these questions is most likely, "No!"

Memorize the sentence below. It is the key to brainstorming ideas for unusual ways for making money.

People with money pay other people to do things that they **DON'T** *want to do themselves.*

Scrub a Smelly Can

Scrubbing out a smelly garbage can is a chore almost no one WANTS to do. That is why you can make money doing this job. A good business-person understands that there is no such thing as easy money. Some of the richest people in the world started out cleaning fish, digging up earthworms, or washing dirty dishes at fancy restaurants. So, take a deep breath through your mouth and get started.

Materials
1/8 cup scented liquid dish soap
rubber gloves
1 rag mop
1 high-pressure hose attachment
1 garden hose long enough to reach the
    gutter in the street
1 stepping stool (optional); use to reach
    the inside of tall cans

Directions
1. Carry or pull the *empty* garbage can out to the street gutter.
2. Either use the customer's garden hose or attach your hose to the nearest outdoor faucet and pull the nozzle out to the gutter.
3. Attach the high-pressure nozzle to the hose and fill the can with about four inches of water. *Do not overfill. Water is very heavy.*
4. Pour in the soap.
5. Using the mop, swish the water around until lots of bubbles appear.
6. Wearing gloves, scrub the sides, bottom, and lid of the can with the mop until they are clean.
7. Dump out the water and spray the can with clean water.
8. Dump out the water again and let the can air dry.

**"It takes less time to do a thing right,
than it does to explain why you did it wrong."
—Henry Wadsworth Longfellow**

Activity

13

A Brief History of Windows

MONEY TIP: You won't go through life getting paid for everything you do. When an adult asks you to do something, doing it willingly. If your mom tells you to take out the garbage (and it's not on your chores list), don't ask her how much she will pay you. Just do it!

Early windows were just holes in walls. Over time, people covered the holes with animal hides that had been scraped and stretched very thin. Glass became common in ordinary homes in the early 17th century.

In 1696, William III of England introduced a **window tax**. For every window in your house, you had to pay a certain amount of money to the king. The more windows you had, the more you had to pay.

Poor people who couldn't afford the tax *bricked up* their windows. An open door became their only source of natural light. Those who kept their windows took great pride in them and cleaned them to a brilliant shine each day. This law lasted until 1851, over 150 years.

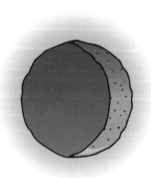 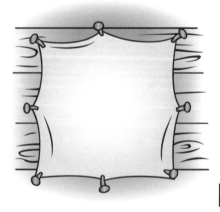 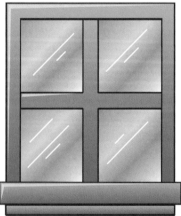

Windows Bright

Housekeepers usually like their windows washed at least once a season. Professional cleaners or an adult without a fear of heights should clean outside windows higher than one story. Children over age eight can easily rub most other windows clean.

Materials
liquid window cleaner concentrate
water
spray bottle
newspaper
rubber gloves
stepping stool (optional); for reaching high
  corners

Directions
1. Put on the rubber gloves.
2. Have an adult help you prepare the cleaning mixture by following the directions on the container.
3. Work inside first.
4. Spray the cleaning mixture on the window. Don't spray too much, or it will form puddles on the windowsill.
5. Crumple up a sheet of newspaper and use it to wipe the window clean.
6. Pay special attention to each corner and along the edges.
7. Go outside and repeat.
8. Look closely for smudges and smears, and remove them with the newspaper.

- Newspaper is cheaper to use than paper towels. Housekeeping experts say the ink in the paper adds shine to a window. Recycle when done.

"Quality means doing it right when no one is looking."
—Henry Ford

Activity
14

Shoveling Snow

MONEY TIP: When customers see that you do a great job of mowing a lawn or quickly clearing a sidewalk after a snowstorm, they will be happy to recommend you to friends. This is called **word of mouth advertising,** and it doesn't cost you a penny.

The greatest snowfall in a 24-hour period in the United States was 76 inches at Silver Lake, Colorado, on April 15, 1921. The most snow to fall in one winter season was at Mount Baker, Washington. An amazing 1,140 inches covered this mountain peak.

Shoveling snow is a seasonal job because it only snows in winter. Even if it did snow on the Fourth of July, the hot weather would return so quickly that your services wouldn't be needed.

- DO pass out index cards with your name and phone number in the fall. Include what you will shovel, such as front walkway and sidewalk or just driveway. Size up the job and charge according to how much area you will need to shovel.

- DON'T sleep late on snowy mornings. Get up before your neighbors need to go to work. Walk up and down the street with your shovel, offering your service. You may be surprised how many people will want to hire you.

Mowing Lawns

In the early 1800s, an Englishman named Edwin Budding invented the first push lawn mower. Before his invention became popular, only wealthy landowners had green lawns around their homes. The grass was cut by workmen using *scythes*, which are sharp, curved knives.

Our earliest U.S. presidents, Washington and Jefferson, were a bit more practical. They let sheep run free on their lawns to chew the grass low to the ground.

Mowing lawns is another seasonal job in most parts of the United States. If you live along the West Coast or in the South, you could get a steady income from just a few customers. But in most places, mowing lawns is summer work.

- DO learn how to use a push mower or power mower by practicing at home.
- Exchange use of the family mower by mowing your own lawn once a week for FREE.
- DO NOT use a power edger if you are under the age of 12. Team up with an older friend to get the job done, or tell the customer that edging is not included in the job. Those tools can be dangerous.
- ALWAYS sweep up the walks after mowing.

> **"I always thought a yard was three feet long; then I started mowing the lawn."**
> **—C. E. Cowan**

Activity 15

What's a Weed?

> **MONEY TIP:** Brainstorm catchy names for whatever service you are offering. Instead of printing **Weeding** across the top of your index card, try **Speedy Weedy** or **Wanted: Weeds.**

Gardeners are fond of saying, "What is one man's weed is another man's flower." This means that one gardener might want every bit of milkweed dug out of her garden, while the gardener next door thinks milkweed is beautiful because it is a home for monarch butterflies. Actually, the definition of a weed is *a plant that grows where it is not wanted.*

- You will need to know what each customer calls a weed.
- Work side by side with each gardener at first, only pulling up those plants that she or he calls a weed.
- If you are unsure about a plant, *ask.*
- After a few sessions you will grow confident and be able to weed on your own.

Deadheading

There are two types of flowering plants. One type is an **annual**. Annuals only live for one season. They produce loads of colorful blooms and then die. The other type is a **perennial**. These plants stay alive year after year, blooming at different times from spring to fall. Both types of plants stay healthier and produce more blooms longer if you **deadhead** them.

Deadheading sounds like something out of a horror movie, but it is really quite a pleasant job. Plants make seeds as their flowers die. Once a plant has made enough seeds, it takes a rest and goes on vacation. In other words, it stops blooming.

The dying flowers of a plant are called *heads*. Deadheading is the task of pinching or clipping off the dying flowers before they make seeds. It's best done either before the day gets too hot or in the evening near sunset.

Materials
gardening gloves
small clippers that fit well in your hand
small bucket
hat and/or sunblock

Directions
1. Always wear a hat and/or cover your neck, ears, and face with sunblock.
2. Ask your customer which plants to deadhead.
3. Use your fingertips or the clippers to nip the dying flower off. Remove as little of the stem as possible.
4. NEVER cut off entire sections or branches. Deadheading needs to be done *one flower at a time*.

"Whatever you have, spend less."
—Samuel Johnson

Activity
16

Falling Leaves

MONEY TIP: Contact the secretary at a local school or church. Ask if you can place a short note about your new business in their weekly newsletter.

As fall approaches, the temperature outside begins to drop, and the days get shorter. The shorter days signal trees that produce leaves to stop making chlorophyll. *Chlorophyll* (klor-o-fill) is the substance that makes a leaf green.

Once leaves stop making chlorophyll, they lose their green color. What is left are glorious golds, magnificent reds, splendid yellows, and eye-popping oranges that color the fall landscape.

Leaves left in piles can cause a lot of damage. Lawns buried under wet leaves grow white mold. Leaf-filled rain gutters clog during storms, and sewers back up into basements. As the first snowflakes drift toward the ground, leaf-covered streets become slick and dangerous.

Someone needs to rake up all those leaves. It might as well be you.

Gathering Leaves

People have many methods for gathering fallen leaves. The tools you must have are leaf bags and a strong, lightweight, close-tined rake. Below are some inventive ideas to make this job easier:

- Go over the leaves with a power mower that has a mulching function and a self-bagger. Then, use the rake to finish up the job.
- Use a leaf sucker; it vacuums up the leaves. The problem for kids is that they are heavy and noisy. If you use one, wear earplugs.
- Work with a friend. Rake up the leaves together. Then, have one person hold the leaf bag open while the other shovels in the leaves. Switch jobs for the next bag.
- Take time to laugh. See if you can create the tallest pile of leaves in the neighborhood. Jumping on it helps squish down the leaves, and most people agree that it's great fun.

"If money is all a man makes, then he will be poor. Poor in happiness and poor in all the things that make life worth living."
—Herbert N. Casson

Activity
17

Other Yard Jobs

MONEY TIP: Ask your parents if you can have a small patch of ground for planting vegetables or fresh herbs. When the produce is ready to harvest, pick it and seal it in resealable plastic bags. Stick on colorful labels that describe the contents and how much each bag costs. Now you have something different than lemonade to sell.

Snails and slugs are two common garden pests. Leaving behind a shiny, slimy trail, they slide around vegetable and flower beds at night, on cloudy days, and in the early morning. The "early bird who gets the worm" also likes to munch on an occasional snail or two. However, even a whole flock of birds would have a hard time ridding a garden of snails. *Snail busting* is a perfect kid's job!

- Did you know that snails have four noses? Wear garden gloves if you are squeamish about touching slimy things.
- Look for snails early in the morning or right after a rainstorm. Gardeners often use flashlights and go out on snail searches at night.
- ALWAYS throw snails away in a plastic bag with a knot tied at the top. Snails are escape artists. If a snail is left alive, it can crawl out of anything but sealed plastic bags and bottles with screw-on lids.

Don't sprinkle salt on snails and watch them melt. It does kill the snail, but the salt is *very harmful* to the plants in the garden.

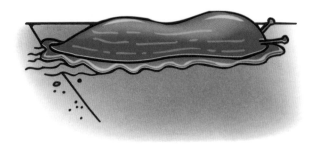

Wind Fruit

Most fruit grown on trees in urban (city) spaces is never picked. Over the growing season, the fruit falls to the ground, attracting flies and wasps. Eventually, it turns into a sticky, soggy mess. There are several ways to make money from these trees.

1. Offer to pick your neighbors' fruit as it ripens. In early summer, apricots are ready first, followed quickly by cherries. Mid-summer you will find pears, plums, and peaches. Apples are usually ready to be picked by September, and late fall brings walnuts, pecans, and chestnuts.

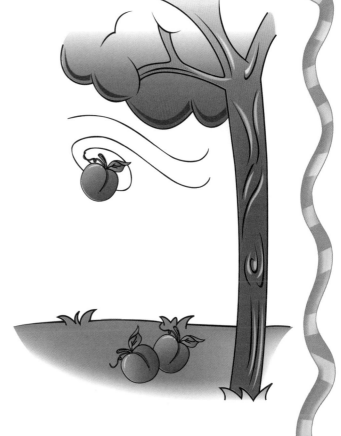

2. **Wind fruit** is fruit that has blown to the ground on a windy day. Right after a windstorm, ask your neighbors if they'd like to hire you to pick up this fruit. Ask if you can take it home. If you are lucky, the answer will be, "Yes!" Use the fruit to make jam or fruit leather. Or sell it to passing drivers from your front curb.

   You have now made money twice from the same fruit—once for picking it up and once by making it into something yummy and selling it.

3. Other than wind fruit, most fruit that falls to the ground is *too rotten* to use. A customer might want this fruit shoveled onto a compost pile or simply thrown away.

"If you can actually count your money, then you are not a rich man."
—J. Paul Getty, billionaire

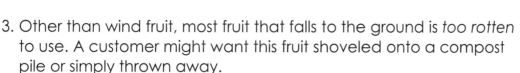

Activity

18

Anyone Can Paint a Fence

MONEY TIP: Instead of spending your money on birthday or holiday gifts, give a chore coupon. Design a coupon for the chore you will do, place it in a small box, and wrap it with paper and sparkly ribbons. Some ideas are washing your dad's car, giving your mom a 20-minute foot massage, or painting your grandparents' fence. Write down four more ideas.

_____   _____

_____   _____

Mark Twain wrote a famous description about fence painting in *The Adventures of Tom Sawyer.*

"Tom appeared on the sidewalk with a bucket of whitewash and a long-handled brush. He surveyed the fence and all gladness left him... Thirty yards of fence nine feet high."

If you have read the story, you know that Tom tricks the boys from town by pretending that painting a fence is an important and interesting job. The happier Tom seems, the more the town boys want a chance to paint the fence. Soon, Tom is resting under an elm tree, eating an apple and watching others do his work.

The boys traded their treasures for the chance to paint Tom's fence. You can trade your work for money by doing some outdoor painting yourself.

Paint Like Michelangelo

Indoor painting requires a professional or someone who is skilled at preparing the walls and woodwork before the first coat of paint goes on. Painting outdoor fences is not so difficult. It usually just requires time. There's no better place to learn how to paint than on a neighbor's fence.

Materials
mixed paint and paintbrushes supplied by the customer
overalls or old shirt
old newspaper and rocks or tape (optional)
sunblock and/or hat

Directions
1. Cover your clothes with an old shirt or overalls. Apply sunblock to any exposed skin.
2. Have an adult open the can of well-mixed paint.
3. Cover any cement or brick at the base of the fence with newspaper and secure with rocks or tape.
4. Dip about 1/3 of the brush into the paint. Wipe off any excess along the inside rim of the can.
5. Stroke the brush smoothly up and down along the fence boards, catching any drips.
6. Repeat until done or until, like Tom Sawyer, you can get someone else to do your work.

"If a man is called a streetsweeper, he should sweep streets even as Michelangelo painted, or Beethoven composed music, or Shakespeare wrote poetry. He should sweep streets so well that all the hosts of Heaven and Earth will pause to say, 'Here lived a great streetsweeper who did his job well.'"
—Martin Luther King, Jr.

Activity
19

Buenos Días

MONEY TIP: Save money by using your local library. Besides books, you can check out CDs, DVDs, and videotapes. If you want to sit a while, you can read the latest issues of your favorite magazines.

- The United States of America has never declared English as its official language.
- 176 languages are spoken in the United States.
- A *heritage speaker* is a person who speaks English but lives in a home where a language other than English is spoken.

The top 10 most spoken languages in the United States are

English	215 million	Tagalog	1.2 million
Spanish	28 million	Vietnamese	1.1 million
Chinese	2 million	Italian	1 million
French	1.6 million	Korean	900,000
German	1.4 million	Russian	700,000

(Tagalog is the official language of the Philippines.)

Tutoring a Foreign Language

One of the hardest parts about learning a foreign language is getting enough practice *speaking* it. Children who immigrate (move from another country) to the United States are often shy when they start school. These children rarely speak English. At recess, they find other children who speak their language. After school, they return to homes where they often do not speak English. These children need more time practicing English.

Children who only speak English also have a hard time learning a new language. They might take classes at school in Spanish, Chinese, French, Italian, or German, but they have almost no chance to practice speaking the language *outside* of class.

- Children make excellent tutors for other children.
- If you speak English and want to tutor non-English speaking children, ask your teachers at school to help you identify those students who could use your services.
- If you speak more than one language, check out the foreign language classes in your school for students who might need help.

To help others learn, you can read foreign language picture books out loud. Point to objects in magazines and say their names. Everyone learns a language by first naming things like *ball, dog*, and *cat*. Then they start describing them: *red ball, big dog, fat cat*. Finally, they make sentences: "I want the red ball." "I see a big dog." "Don't feed the fat cat." Mostly, just let the child you are helping practice, practice, and practice.

"A mile is walked one step at a time."
—Unknown

Activity

20

Read and Listen

MONEY TIP: Toddlers can be very hard on books. They rip pages, chew corners, and scribble with crayon. Call your local library to see if they have a yearly book sale. These sales often allow you to buy books for mere pennies. Dig through the children's picture books and buy the ones that are in really good shape. Resell them to neighborhood families with toddlers who don't want to buy new books only to have them ruined.

If you hand a book to a child who has never seen one, she might look at it upside down. Instead of starting at the front, she might start at the back. And certainly, the letters will have no meaning.

By the age of eight, most children in the United States can read simple books. They have learned the alphabet, and they understand that the letters C-A-T put together spell the word CAT.

Reading experts tell parents to read to their children for at least 20 minutes every day. They also tell parents to have their children read aloud. Like everything in life, it is impossible to really learn any skill if you don't practice. You might be able to help a child practice and make money doing it.

42 million adult Americans read so poorly they can't understand the front page of a newspaper.

The Magic of Books

Reading to a child or listening to a child read is a nice, steady after-school job. *Offering to meet the child outside a classroom and walk home together might increase what you can ask for payment.*

The In-Home Reader/Listener

- The parents or guardian of the child should provide the books you are to read.
- Read aloud for 20 minutes in a quiet, comfortable place. If the child has begun to read, take turns reading and listening.
- ALWAYS have the child look at the page as you read. Point to the words as you say them. Stop here and there to have the child talk about the pictures.
- Listen to what the child says and ask open-ended questions. Open-ended questions can't be answered with yes or no. "What is that character doing?" is an open-ended question.

The Library Reader

- See if your library has a room where you could hold a group read-aloud session once or twice a week.
- Keep the group size small (3–8). Use lots of expression in your voice.
- Borrow the read-aloud books from the library and practice beforehand. Don't forget to show the pictures to the group and give them time to see them well.

Activity
21

Does It Have to Be Lemonade?

MONEY TIP: Sell hot chocolate on cold fall days when your neighbors are out raking up leaves. Instead of a stand, put your supplies in a wagon and sell house-to-house.

Lemons are a citrus fruit that came from northern India. Two thousand years ago, a bright yellow lemon with a thick peel was the perfect fruit. As long as the lemons were kept dry, a trader could transport them long distances, and the lemons would not rot.

Lemons were called "golden apples." Sellers at market would shout out the wonderful things a lemon could do. A lemon could preserve and flavor other foods. Doctors used lemons to heal skin wounds. Mixed with water or wine, lemons made a healthy drink that prevented a deadly disease called *scurvy*.

Lemons were so valuable that they were traded for fine cloth, precious metals, and slaves. Along with figs, lemons were packed in crates and sent to Turkey, Pakistan, Iran, and Eastern Europe to be bought by wealthy families.

Nowadays, kids set up lemonade stands to make money in the summer. But lemonade isn't the only thing you can sell.

Make Your Sign Big

If you sell anything from a stand—lemonade, cold water, vegetables, fruit, iced tea—make sure your sign is readable from at least a half-block away.

- Drivers need to pay attention to the road, not to itty-bitty signs. If your sign is tiny, they won't know what you are selling until they have driven **past your sign**. Most drivers don't turn around.
- Use bright **primary** colors on your sign and keep it simple. Write what you are selling and how much. Nothing more!
- Place your stand where drivers can stop their car out of the way of traffic.

Be creative when setting up a drink stand!
- Sell something besides artificially flavored, sugary drinks. Maybe people would like 100% fruit juice frozen on a wooden stick?
- Slightly sweetened iced teas, either black or herbal, are refreshing on hot summer days.
- Sell bottled water bought at deep-discount stores and frozen until the water is slushy.

> **"When life give you lemons, make lemonade."**
> —Unknown

Activity
22

Activity

23

Do I Have Mail?

MONEY TIP: Volunteering your time can sometimes lead to a paying job. Places such as churches, food banks, community gardens, and schools use lots of volunteers to keep everything running. If you show that you are a good worker by doing what you promised to do, the organization might offer to pay you to do even more work.

Offer to weed a community garden, and next year you might be paid to organize the whole weeding crew. Help teach the toddlers their Sunday school lessons, and by the time you are twelve your church might pay you a little each week to teach the first graders.

Ask your parents if you can look at the mail they get for a couple of weeks. Look at all the envelopes that contain a letter. How many have been stamped with a regular "stuck-on" stamp? Have any of them been addressed by hand?

Each year in the United States businesses and organizations send out millions of pieces of mail that have been stuffed, addressed, and stamped *by hand*. *By hand* means a machine did not do the job. If you can fold a piece of paper, know where to stick an address label, or can lick a stamp, you can make some money.

Stuff, Lick, and Send

Right now, someone is planning a big fund-raising event. They will need hundreds, or even thousands, of invitations mailed out. Businesses send out advertisements for special sales, bills, or notices that they are moving to a new address. These people often need someone who is willing to work and meet a deadline. A **deadline** is a date when something must be finished. For example, if a local grocery store is having a sale on February 2nd, it would do no good to get the advertising flyer in the mail on February 3rd.

- Ask your parents and their friends to tell you about any fund-raising events they hear about. Contact the organization before they send out their invitations.
- A young couple getting married might be thrilled to pay you to help with the wedding invitations. The bride is usually in charge of this part of the plans.
- Teachers are always putting lesson packets together. This is a time-consuming job, as papers need to be put in order and then stapled. Give them your business card.
- If a post office is nearby, offer to make trips to mail packages and pick up stamps for people. The elderly, parents with young children, and local businesses are people who might use this service.

"I have enough money to last me the rest of my life, unless I buy something."
—Jackie Mason

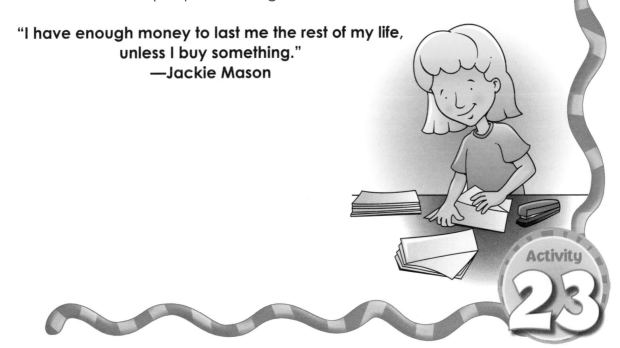

Activity
23

What Is the Stock Market?

> **MONEY TIP:** Kids can buy stock just like anyone else. The time to start learning about the stock market is as soon as you can understand basic math and read a newspaper. The younger you are when you begin to buy stock, the longer you will have to let your investment grow.

The **stock market** can seem overwhelming, so you should think about it *a little at a time*. It's like learning a new language, and it will take practice for you to understand.

Let's start with some important terms:

Stock: Businesses need money to buy supplies and pay workers. Some businesses sell stock, or **shares** of their company, to make money. Suppose Mr. Black owned the Red Racing Bicycle Company and decided he needed to raise some money to buy more bicycles. Mr. Black could sell you a share, or part, of his company. That would make you a part owner of his business. Then, when the Red Racing Bicycle Company made money, you would make money.

Profit: The money a business makes after paying its bills is called a profit.

Dividend: A company makes a profit if it makes more money than it spends. It pays the part-owners cash from this profit. This payment is called a dividend. The more shares you own in a company, the more you are paid.

- Many companies will sell you one share of their business. At first, you will own just a teeny bit of the company. But if you keep buying stock in the same company, one day you just might own the whole thing!

Let's Play the Stock Market

Unlike putting your money in a savings account, buying shares in a company has some risk. Money in savings accounts will always make money over time. The growth might be slow, but there is little chance that you will lose money.

On the other hand, while a company might make a profit, it could also lose money. If it loses money, you, the "part-owner," will also lose money. All businesses have ups and downs. There are times when they make lots of money and times when they lose money. Be patient, and over a period of about ten years you should see your investment grow.

So, why buy stocks instead of putting all your money in a savings account? Well, one reason is that the value of stocks can grow much faster. A wise plan is to have money in both.

Here is a safe way to learn how the stock market works. Pretend you have $100 to invest. Choose a company that makes or does something you like and sells stock. Look up the company's stock symbol on the Internet or in the newspaper. Decide how many shares you can "buy." Then use the graph on the next page to follow the company's stock price for two weeks. Record the price each day. Are your shares worth more than they were when you started tracking them? Are they worth less? Did you make money?

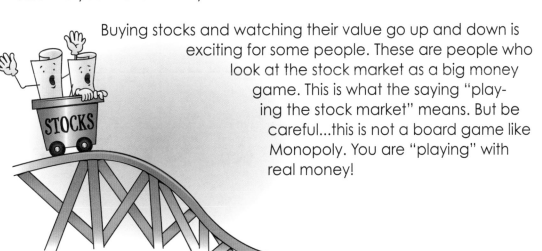

Buying stocks and watching their value go up and down is exciting for some people. These are people who look at the stock market as a big money game. This is what the saying "playing the stock market" means. But be careful...this is not a board game like Monopoly. You are "playing" with real money!

Activity
24

Price **Stock**_____ **Date** _____ to _____

Start—

M T W Th F M T W Th F